Love-in-a-mist

Poems by Anne Connolly

Red Squirrel Press
(Scotland)

First published in the UK in 2011 by
Red Squirrel Press (Scotland)

Red Squirrel Press (Head Office)
Holy Jesus Hospital
City Road
Newcastle upon Tyne
United Kingdom
NE1 2AS
www.redsquirrelpress.com

Red Squirrel Press is represented by Inpress Ltd.
www.inpressbooks.co.uk

Copyright © Anne Connolly 2011

The right of Anne Connolly to be identified as the author
of this work has been asserted by her in accordance with
the Copyright, Designs and Patents Act of 1988.
All rights reserved.

A CIP catalogue record is available from the British Library
ISBN: 978-1-906700-44-7

Printed by Martins the Printers
Sea View Works
Spittal
Berwick upon Tweed
United Kingdom
TD15 1RS

for Mike

Contents

(to be continued)	7
Begun	8
Belly dancing	10
Next past the post	11
Job description	12
Rewoven	13
A good neighbour	14
Maundy Thursday	15
Revision	16
O fiore della passione	17
Changing room	18
Role call	19
The fascination of toes	20
Soot-prints	21
Nativity	22
Chivalry	24
Croque mort	25
Craft	26
Forward slash/doped linen	28
H....E.R.-.O-----	29
Handler	30
Reserved occupation	32
The siege of Sarajevo	33
Stailc ocrais-Hunger strike	34
Lament of the Omagh twins	36
Mean time	37
So much for the cease-fire	38
17th March 2003	40
Shanti, síocháin, shalom	42
Some fields are missing	43
Gabh mo leithscéal-Sorry	44

Love-in-a-mist	46
Named	48
The song of the Gansey	49
Master class-Glasgow docks	51
The understanding of drink	52
The scale of things	53
E-male	54
Loose change	55
Mouth to mouth	56
Pearls	57
Last call	58
Eschatology for aspiring escapologists	59
Balance	60
The long haul	61
Portal dolmen	62
Paperwork	63
Into care	64
Curtain call	65
ICU	66
Dry rot	67
Lia Fáil	68
Glen Lyon	69
Ogham	70
Troon ferry	71
Mahee Island	72
Early doors	74
Cold night in Tromso	75
Arles	76
Image	77
Shall we dance?	78
Owed to poets	79
Astrolabe	80
Orbit	81

Part One

(to be continued)

Children's children cannot be explained
except to say it's being young again
in the very core of the apple
before it is picked, eaten, ready
to scatter, seed the earth
like welcome rain.

Begun

Little one just begun
multiplying and dividing,
hide in the helix of your worth
count on still-to-be fingers that birth
will be the outcome of your growing.
So much knowing now. Blueprints
filled with plus and minus balance
the sum of your small life.
In vitro veritas. Perhaps. A burst
of joy when you first plant your future,
trigger starts and stops to your unique
conclusion. You are the fruit nurtured
by great longing. Is it wrong to tell
that cryo-siblings wait just in case
you fail the scrutiny of science?
At what cost
  will they defrost
    your sister
      or your brother?
        Ask your father
          and your mother
            little one just begun
              multiplying and dividing.

We are afraid of the pain
of your pain. Better
not have to bear
the incalculable
burden.
No one's gain.
Genetic jinx, chinks
in the chains that link
could bring us all
to zero.

I am the
ampersand
of self to self
the start of
ever-
being.

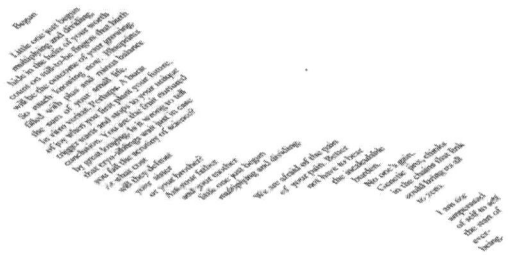

Belly dancing

Even if I had the figure and the vigour too
I would not choose to be a belly dancer
because, much as I savour the energy
of hip and thigh and foot lunging
or thrusting to the rhythm, swaying
hypnotic with the least vibration
of vivid beads controlled by artfulness
around my belly's dome
I could not hide the scar where
surgical precision slashed me through
appendix to ectopic tube in one left swish,
a masterpiece of stitching up my life,
a watermark that guarantees maternity
of our third child, the one that lives
on the brink of memory until I think
of my belly dancing, lunging and thrusting
to the rhythm of small feet and hands
that never thumped me awake at night
from that warm cavern underneath the heart.

Next past the post

I tatted out the mane
of the horse his father rode
trotting to the fair
with me and Moll Maloney
on a jaunty Irish air.

The years were teased, tugged
from flanks and ears
wood rubbed clean as a first-
day-at-school boy.

Foetal heart beat raced
lickety-spit well past the post
Epidural only half way there

contractions sharper
than an obstetrician's knife
scrubbed up and ready
for the gallop against fifty-fifty

till the bawl went up
louder than a rugby cheer
and the rockers steadied
ready for the next ride.

Job description

Enthusiastic
Innovative
Motivated

To work with women
Undergoing both first and second
Trimester terminations

Amniocentesis
Spina bifida
Downs syndrome

We are an equal opportunities employer
Positive about applicants with disabilities.

(Glasgow Herald 18.02.1999)

Rewoven

Belly half-full with would-be Jack she ran
away; never looked back to see her brother
in constabulary mode blaze with righteous rage
at sister's boldness. Loss of face. Loss of faith.
A papish stable hand broke her in, fractured
the Sabbath of that narrow Ulster town.

Every wave heaved and lurched to Glasgow.
Cobbles rougher than sea paved disenchantment.
No wedding ring or diadem of flowers. No toast
to years of plenty. Sleep half-full of waking
marked the winnowing; smell of father's horse
new-shod, heady summer of the hayfield, sour
breath of beer and privy full of yesterday.

Yet he was warm beside her, smile still tender
when the tide was fair and his unerring eye
for sturdy haunch and well-turned fetlock
saw them through another season and the price home.
Four sons the tally and a tomboy girl. My mother.
We heard the tale, romantic, tuned to a fine morality.
The Web untangles truth. Shakes out old bones.

A good neighbour

She had no children, borrowed us
from time to time, made pinkie tea
and cakes that wouldn't feed a fairy.
All her chairs had ruffled bits
to keep the arm-rests clean, a divil
for the fidget of a girl I always was
and strangely called, or so I thought,
after some aunt, McCasser or that ilk
who like herself embodied neatness.

We knew that she was very, very old,
pink scalp a sweep of dandelion puffs
as light as dreaming. Our mother
told us she was prematurely grey
from some uncommon ailment
that involved whispers, odd looks
and mysteries of womanhood.

Her man could tell a winner in a blink,
the tilt of the head and sinewed thigh,
clear eye and glossy coat furrowed with ribs
he'd calculated to the last ounce of offal.
Owners carted them from all across the North
to hear how they might shorten odds
and fleece the wealthy bookies.

Greyhounds were his livelihood, paid
for all the figurines and unworn carpets
that he loved her with and in return
she sewed the linen altar cloths in gold
and silver Latin - Mater Misericordiae.

Maundy Thursday

No bells tonight.
Only the altar-boys,
red cassocks, immaculate albs,
swinging the clappers
over and over
to show the time is near.

And Benedict effectively has said
"I am innocent
of the broken souls
of boys like these,"
washed his hands
after the desecration,
clasped his hands tight
around the reputation of Peter.

Greater love than this is why
the broken body still hangs high
on each Good Friday. Hear them cry
Pie Jesu Domine.

Revision

To be back there in corridors he knew
with nothing to be afraid of - uncanny
and the roll-call unravelling in his head,
some names already carved in memoriam.
Up there behind the hand-ball wall boys fought
and smoked and said *fuck* in bold italics,
ducked the radar eye of Brother Michael
who lost his ability for applied mathematics
when it came to seven-of-the-best.

Above the sunlit place where they walked
a calvary scene rose ten times smaller
than his memory. Mary's face was paler
than the death of her son and he thought
of the wrench that came on an April morning
aged thirteen when his own mother slept on
into eternity. This place was no place
                for mothers.

O fiore della passione

Satin-white ironstone, Grindley of Staffordshire
tutu of tissue frothed around each one.

Deep draw of Kensitas
counting coupons
into neat hundreds
puff puff till the tally
smoke-ringed his target of six
and the table's set.
No more need for seven.

Passion flowers stylized on the deep curved rim,
pale greenery to lure the taste buds in to Sunday dinner.

With our mother gone
in a swift stitch-up
of the heart,
arteries closed tight
like underwater breath
held far too long
we needed ritual.

He chose them. Not flamboyant roses or forget-me-nots
or mottled harlequin to colour up the grim extraction
of her life from
everything we knew
but o fiore della passione.

Changing room

A space to lay down
the kicking screaming infant
wipe up the shit and spew
accumulated while you tried
to shop and gradually
there is room to cuddle,
feed, pat-a-cake rhythm
on the sticky little back, floppy,
stroke the unsteady head,
fontanelle still thumping
fragile and generous with life
till the thought of changing
your baby for the magazine version
you almost believed
was going to squawk its way
from the delivery room
into ordered days and nights
of record-book proportions,
the thought itself is changed
and hung out to dry.

Role Call

Midwife, wipe her clean and cut the pulsing cord.

Teacher, lead her out with numbers, thoughts and words.

Doctor, heal her well in body and in mind.

Play-mate, laugh and tease, coax, adventure and be kind.

Work-mate, greet and help her put in an honest day.

Priest, be there to nourish with God along the way.

Soul-mate, find and keep her, remember love is made.

Everyone who meets her be open, not afraid.

Children, if she bears you do not forget the gift.

Reader, if you are a man just change these words to fit.

The fascination of toes

Sit by the back door
listen to warm summer rain
the rhythm and the soft swish of it.
No sense to this sound, no boundaries
beyond cloud and the thirst of earth.
You quieten, grab the fascination of toes,
click your tongue. Today's new trick.

You seem to know there's something big
out there, falling through air and light
and time and our afternoon visit,
while Ma-ma says goodbye to an old friend.
Twenty eight years of someone else's son.

Soot-prints

Outside pale mallow is still in bloom
opened all the way to the topmost buds.
December wind is tossing, tossing, but
branches will be pliant for another while,
frail, defiant in the face of snow.
It's there in the pewter pink of clouds
that forecast better than computers.

Inside, his small head is resting on my chest,
replete while his exhausted mother steals
what sleep she can in these earliest of days.
Who knows what games this tiny fellow
plays throughout his snuffling, suckling-
what dreams his parents have for him
after the long haul of childhood?

Our father hunkered down to pattern soot-prints
round the hearth on Christmas Eve
crouched over old boots that gardened,
caught up clay by the patch of summer mint
where chewing gum sprang up overnight
white on aromatic sprigs strong enough
to launch the flight of our imagination.

Nativity

Joe the joiner watched his baby
lying in the straw
smelt the sweat and afterbirth
hoped the night would thaw
lay by his exhausted wife
the proudest man on earth
dreamt of how he'd teach the boy
what wood and nails are worth.

Part two

Chivalry

At Agincourt before they fought
men bent and kissed the ground.
Each ate a morsel of the earth
as eucharist and silent requiem
perhaps for dust to dust might be
the sacrament of soil that bound
them man to man with even enemy.

They could not tell that rank
by stinking rank they'd count
as heroes. Worn down by dysentery
they floundered breechless
in the late autumnal rain,
battered a treachery of stakes
deep into the mud till horse and man
became a skewered hysteria of sound.

Then fear disgraced all mercy,
stirred a new-found appetite
for captive blood and deeds
that ever after squandered sleep
while heralds blew their notes,
declared for God and Harry.

Croque mort

Will you undertake
to bite the dead?
Let your teeth
and inadvertently
your lips and tongue
grip and close firm
in that strange kiss?

Purpled with plague
livid with the long march
into the embrace of enemies
these feet have danced
and skipped, tangled
in the weave of lovers' play
only a day or two ago.

But on the battlefield
and in the carts piled high
with "Bring out your dead"
only the living flinch.

Ours is the watermark of pain
that cannot brand the man
who's stepped into eternity.
No amuse-bouche this gnawing.
You must have the taste for it.

(Croque mort - undertaker)

Craft

He has shown us
   how to pleat
      six yards of cloth
         methodical and neat
            without the urgency
               of winter morning,
                  measured knee to heel
                     for fit and comfort
                        pouched according to the need
                           for forage, food and barter.

A scian dubh
   could bleed enough
      for oatmeal mixed
         and cooked on hot stone
            or pierce a fresh hide
               to tongue and lace against
                  the rugged edge of Scotland.

He has told us
   how they clarted
      up their blades
         with dirt and dung
            to fester enemies
               on the slow road to dying.

I take the chance to lift
   and hold a broadsword
      muscles shocked at the load
         the blatant double-edge
            of slaughter cleaved deep
               when any man sank to the calf
                  betrayed by chainmail armour
                  and lame strategy.

Culloden field sodden with the dead
   to Helmand Province crushed
      as worn-out poppies -
         tonight I have pleated up
            the warmth of tradition
               held the chill of it
                  in my own two hands.

Forward slash/doped linen

Men argue about doped linen.
It changes with the subtle switch of light
from faded honeyed cream to translucent
white when you look up at the wings.
That's why the Germans called their plane
"The Dove"- prototype of stealth unseen
when flown above twelve hundred feet.
Neat. It must have scared the goggles off
the enemy, those boys with cashmere chins
who'd only just learned to swagger.

The fact is that dope perished. Cracked
in the strong ultra-violet swoop and glide.
Gathered death and life in weft and woof.
Swathes fell away, fluttered like discarded
pinions as the German pilots dived.

If making a model remember prizes always
swing towards authenticity. The Taube
was first inspired by the stable drifting of liana
seeds, the ones that slow-spin on a single wing.
Rendition flights can be just as invisible.
Indeed it's how they work that really matters.
The colour of the dope is academic.

H . . . . E . R . - . O - - - - -

He saw the Spitfires bank, flame
over the Forth, knew the urge
to be a hero. So he grew a bit
enlisted on the dot of sixteen
and left by the Clyde, gliding out
beyond the sheltered neck of water,
stood to attention on the top deck
bound for manhood and Archangel.

Abandon ship! Filled to the gunnels
with necessity, lifeblood of convoy PQ17.
But not before the vital codes were scuppered,
hauled over tilting sides in three great chests
each one heavier than a sodden corpse.

>Intermittent taps
>staccato breaths
>refrigerated marrow
>dot-dash-splash
>pneu-mon-iaaaaaaaaaaaaa.
>
>a long slow haul to
>Bletchley Park.

(Jim Osler was eventually posted to Scotland where he kept in contact with Resistance fighters in Norway.)

Handler

Alone all night listening.
Huge sets glistened with ariels
caught the changing codes.
Lyra held by the Gestapo
hoping to pluck her tune,
Skylark…..wings clipped
on a dying note.

The touch was everything-
instant recognition
like a sneeze in church.
But Venus' wife perfected him,
held the echo of his love
in slim fingers, lying to the tips
of nails ragged with anxiety
for two whole months.
A faint V-sign and a small hurray
crowned her persistent symphony.
Not dead, not dead, not dead.

Mine were a litany of gods
and stars clustered
        in the far North.

                        Brunehilde

              Odin   Pisces

                   Aquila

                                   Bilor

                      Bjorn

                    Randi

            Uullflax

Njord

Reserved occupation

She could have been a clever engineer.
Had the brain but not the inclination.

> So she used her
> long, long legs,
> blonde, blonde hair,
> blue, blue eyes
>
> and well-articulated hips
> to join the Windmill.
> Kept the world birling.

The siege of Sarajevo

In Sarajevo a man sold cigarette puffs,
ordinary life sucked deeply in,
a momentary fix of memory.
He had the pleasure in between
punters, no overheads and yet
who could resent such ingenuity?

I salute his style maintaining cool
just like the mothers buying bread
who ran the gauntlet in high heels
wine-red lipstick splashed on mouths
poised to spit at bombs and snipers.

Someone said that every day a cellist
bowed his soul out in the city's heart
strung mellow notes of his normality
while blood dried darkly on the pavement
and gunmen played slow Bosnian roulette.

Stailc ocrais-hunger strike

"I am awaiting the lark for spring is all but upon us." Bobby Sands 1981

In the Maze in the grip of it
and he's holding tighter
than the dream of Saoirse
bearing Green and White
and Gold in bloodied arms.

He knows the world is listening
counting statistics of his skinny
clapped-in sides, collapsing veins.
The pain. Christ, only you could
measure it into this near stupor.

But in the deep belly of his being
lies the answer to it all -
the womb of Mother-tongue
the law of Mother-land
the sweep of blue hills
from Fair Head in Antrim
to Mizen Head in Cork-
the longest walk in Ireland.

And why shouldn't a man
of twenty seven common years
have the chance to stray down
alleys of contentious history
with a neighbour who has lost
the appetite for Red, White, Blue?

No more bullets for breakfast.
No more Molotov cocktails
to settle the bile of the day.
Your own shirt on your own back
while you wait for the first lark to sing.

Saoirse - Freedom

Lament of the Omagh twins

They did not count us
those waiting to be born
almost there till we were
spilled and shattered.

Twenty nine plus two
as real as the IRA
we nestled in the warm
 jostled for our own space

joggled in the darkness
to the rhythm of our
mother's walk, talk, laugh
scream in Omagh town

on Market Street, herded
by unadmitted lies
and careless cowards
to the edge of chaos,

afterbirth of history
where kings still ride
on gable ends daubed
with the fractals of fear.

Mean time

Good Friday '98.
They all meant it,
some reluctant still
till the last flick
of the pen.
Omagh
a ghastly
punctuation-
exclamation
question
definitely
not a full stop.
For now they say
disenchanted
boys grow sinister
with old ignorance,
clench a green fist
or red hand
ready to notch
a clear conscience
on a dusty gun.
History is
a twisted tune.
The bodhran skin
could stretch as easy
on a Lambeg drum.

So much for the cease-fire.

We'll give him a six-pack.
Ankles *bang-bang*
knee-caps *bang-bang*
elbows *bang-bang*.
To go any higher would
kill him *bang-bang*
and our cohort might question
the justice *bang-bang*.

But he's gone past the mark
selling drugs in the dark
for a joy-ride of highs
that our system despises,
degrades the high-rises
and counterfeits shame
when we find he's to blame.

We gave him a warning
a house-call one morning.
The beating came next.
He knew what to expect
as we care for our own
and he had to be shown.

He avoided them all
as he pedalled the Falls
till his cover was blasted
by mothers who tasted
the stink of life wasted
without a just cause
like freedom and language,
autonomous laws.

So this is the sound
of pay-time *bang-bang*
no reason or pleading
to save him *bang-bang*
for he's fed on the carrion
left by the past.
Young men and women
whose future is cast
in the spiral of bondage
that's poverty's cage.
That's why we still rage.

17th March 2003

On Slemish mountain plateau
the boy grips a blackthorn stick
head whittled like a swan's neck
bowing to the sun, a crozier
to draw back the straggled day.

Morning seeps up the damp of night
into leather thongs, a simple sandal
grudged by Milcu, hard-fisted master
if sheep are left to stray too far
from the need of slaughter.

Future pilgrims will seek out
this raw-edged sky-bound place
where, like the boy David,
Patrick looks to the East
and sings psalms to the Lord.

From the loneliness of exile,
*   deliver me*
from the fear of enemies,
*   deliver me*
from the falsehood of power,
*   deliver me*
and keep me in the lea of your love.

On that morning far from home
how can he know the path
that centuries ahead will lend
his name to a clear March day,

when, in a cloud of dark decision
lambs will be prepared for killing
and all the voices bawling NO
will be castrated on the way
to Westminster and Capitol Hill?

Shanti, síocháin, shalom

Hello John, Mr Beatle man,
three decades younger
than my Dad but sharing
in the date he died.

He liked to whistle
couldn't hold a tune
but understood
the rhythm of your song.
He wanted freedom
and tranquillity
for our small broken island
torn as it was
with bullets in the back
and love gone sterile
in the fist of civil war.

If you ever meet beyond
this present, smile
at the gifts you recognise
in the soul of one another.

Whistle, sing, twist and shout
Shanti, Síocháin, Shalom.

Síocháin – Gaelighe for Peace

Some fields are missing

I cannot sign this thing
for every time I try
it's only US states
that scroll and so
Computer says again
some fields are missing.

But that is why I want
to sign this thing
for when I'm driving
by a Caterpillar dozing
on a city centre site
like some rapacious bull
I can recall green fields
and olive trees and homes
where bread rises slowly
on a quiet afternoon.

And then the lads come running
caked in dust and mud
and blood with voices choked
so they can barely say *Shalom*.

Gabh mo leithscéal - Sorry

Two syllables
fall easy on a slip
a momentary aberration
smooth the edge of courtesy
or lurk behind the eyes, weighed
in the scales of advantage,

two syllables
could turn pride
to spit and ashes, split
the infinitives of shame
and consolation,

two syllables
have fumbled
in the mouths of decades
waiting to be uttered
after the staccato
of a bang-bang gun
or the stitch-up of laws
that hem the skirts of justice,

two syllables
might butterfly
the belly of despair
salve the hate that festers
on well-tended ignorance,
narrate the half-story
of forgiveness.

Part Three

Love-in-a-mist

Nigella Damascene.
It's where it grows
on the road
that goes North
to Damascus.

Saul fell heavy
from his horse
along this way,
went doolally
for a few days-
holed up
in Straight Street

blind as any mole;
wrestled his soul
till the scales
flaked away
from his fear.

The last thing
he'd seen
before entangling
darkness,
a pale blue flower
feathered
in a crown of green.

Letters meant to kill
lay tattered,
disarmed
beneath an anguish
of hooves.

Later he sewed tents,
folded seams
between his new
searchings,
pondered the crown
that contradicted
their dream.

Named

Magdala's where it all began-the old stone tower
to catch the eye of the boats as they turned for shore.
Too small for me. A bit vain. Made for something better.

His men smelt of fish and brine and muscled work
a rough bunch chosen for the hardy life he led them.
Peter said they'd all been called. Well so was I.

Sometimes they missed the heart of what he said
which wasn't easy and look at where it led.

Other men, hard-faced, thought they could beat
the heaven out of him and so it seemed.

We wound him well in linen sweet with nard.
His hands and feet, unbearable until you thought
of why.

My village named me, marked me out apart
from the other Marys - his mother old with tears
and Martha's sister, hair a cloth of midnight
to wipe the dust of his day.

It was my name he said in the mute light of morning
cauterised the raw darkness with a promise
waiting to be understood.

The song of the gansey

Clickety ring, clickety ring,
round and round the needles sing
four in a circle and one to dance
nimble over the wool they prance,
a fisher gansey calls them out
to weave their patterns, thin or stout
the loved one knows the gifts they bring
as round and round the needles sing.

For decades long they serve and last
tight to the body, close to the mast

finely knit and proof to wind
oiled and supple like a rind

that smells of sea and fish and man
worn in weather tame or thrawn.

The Humber Star stitched in the sleeve
raised by lads who take their leave

is the heart of the lock-wheel turning steady
voices call as boats make ready,

cables twine and twist and play
wrought like the ropes they haul away.

Lines are baited, mussels shelled
wool in the pinny loosely held

for every lull in the work at home
they craft the patterned herringbone

or zig-zag Filey cliff-tops high
thread the dream of home and dry

while men in fisher ganseys sail
knights of the sea in knitted mail.

Clickety ring, clickety ring,
round and round the needles sing
four in a circle and one to dance
nimble over the wool they prance,
a fisher gansey calls them out
to weave their patterns, thin or stout
the loved one knows the gifts they bring
as round and round the needles sing.

Master class – Glasgow docks

"Young Glasgow Communists ," Ken Currie's "Glasgow Triptych" 1986

These bronzed men, oiled, metallic
hard as rivets in the steel sides of progress
sit and stand on their own argument.

One holds the world ready to burl,
tattoos flexed to cast the ropes
that bind them.

Glasgow unfurls to wheezing notes
coughed into a furnace sunrise.

No bland inheritance to smooth the edge
of their day in this Kapital.

No man overboard for want of a hand
to draw him neatly in.

No role-call in this dawn-class of equals.

The understanding of drink

He was very broad and when I looked up
my uncle's chin was just an old hairbrush
neither beard nor shiny-shaved like daddy's.
His words were gluey, clogged with spit
I could see trickle through the stubble,
slow web of stink, not vomit or stale tea
or the lilac spirit for lighting pale lamps
but altogether nosed, blended, ugly.

My mummy pushed him hard away
and he fell down, rocking backward-forward
on the cold floor till my daddy came
to oxtercog him home to maybe sober.

Sometimes on the sideboard's lowest shelf
there would be ruby port at Christmas
dark and sweet stirred in the pudding
but mostly left beside musky napkins
to grace occasions that I don't recall.
Before my sister's wedding friends came
to leave presents, share a pot of tea
or drop of sherry, not quite frowned upon.

Now I savour Shiraz, spicy and full,
crisp ripe-with fruit Gewutztraminer
the name alone intoxicating
or New World wines besotted with the sun
that ease the taste of memory.

The scale of things

He was so golden,
full of blond beer
and honeyed music.
She played the dark,
a Guinness slip-stream
on the ebonies
that could be grace-notes
or a melancholy minor.

Some early harmonies
soared complex, pure
till the drunken discord
of familiarity went off-key.
So they changed
to uisge beatha
from the same bottle.
Sipped the water of life
together. Slowly.

E-male

She set her firewall against him
        filtered him before the message
              broke
his pixilated face might douse her
        cropped rotated sharp to help
              evoke
hard-driven memories from the mother board.
        Her binary emissions decimate all
              hope
as sly-ware spy-ware I-only-want-to-cry-ware
        cannot kill the Trojan horse's
              joke
and he can taste the acrid ash of love
        that lingers in the ether after
              smoke.

Loose change

The loose change of loving
slips abrasive, rough,
finds the frayed thread
that can't hold the jangle
any more. You can hear
the moment when it falls
uneven, spins and falters;
wonder at the stitch
you couldn't put in time
to bind the perfect synergy.

The exchange rate of love
has always fluctuated
even when tucked safe
beneath the marriage bed.
Interest is a dangerous thing
and such expectation
flaws the very currency
it offers. No win. No fee.
But never ever free.

Mouth to mouth

"By Grand Central Station I sat down and wept" by Elizabeth Smart

Resuscitation of love, a gasp
of lies heady as musk
drawn into the cavities of past desire.
Unbearable fullness.
Your suave lips count prescribed amounts
before each disengagement,
press out the rhythm of a heart
caged in the near-dead bones of hope.
Your handbook is a half-baked
Kama Sutra translated
with dyslexic penitence
onto sheets of stone.
If only there were more maybes
than today, a shift that splits
but doesn't break apart
what never really was our bed-rock.
The possibility of fault-lines,
crazy-paving where small resurrections
might reach out. Thorns and all.

Pearls

"The Honourable Mrs Graham" by Thomas Gainsborough.

This silver gown is exquisite.
See how he has caught the sheen,
but what a time he took to paint
my pearls. His work is very fine
and the man knows quite well
my husband will be satisfied
that I am wearing them with pride.

The artist claims they are the price
of small irritations. Oysters ooze
their soothing milk to no avail
and divers seek their opulence
in strange seas. He says they glow
translucent like the curve of my neck.

If he were not a painter I would call
his words impudent but each day
he strives to capture me somehow
so I must bear this strange intimacy.
His sable brush caresses; I hear it sigh,
whisper, soft as the feather plume
he will resume in detail tomorrow.

Last call

Maybe I won't come,
drop all the inevitables,
inescapables, humdrums
of my everyday
that pass for necessity.

Instead I should phone, text,
write or visit serendipity.
You'll never know quite when.
Then if someone gives me
a long-faced message
of your going, I won't need
to be surprised
at how time has trickled,
promises have snowballed
into unpremeditated lies
to cover trails of inertia.

Or else maybe you won't come–
train, boat, hired car
and almost widow's weeds
grown slowly in anticipation.
Certainly not a worn-out bicycle
that half a life ago
stalled on a country lane
punctured by summer's heat
and mended for a year or so
between.

Eschatology for aspiring escapologists

In the Judgement queue before it splits
in two for horns or wings will there be time
to minimise the screen that blares iniquity,
maximise the moments spent bent
over charitable chequebooks or a child
who couldn't cry because of dehydration?
Will there even be a queue, for don't believers say
that God is timeless, aware of every deed, intent
and consequence, melding "was" and "will be"
into an infinity of NOW?

Maybe it's the Mercy-boat that will float tranquillity
and lullaby each one into eternal sleepy-time.
But what if, in the end the devil takes the hindmost
so it's just a stampede to be at the head of the queue
where Woops! The first shall be last and consequently
old-nicked?

Unless there's a ticky-box for the pragmatic equation
which finally might solve the unknown quantity,
the in-spite-of-everythingness that is love?

Balance

Are you able to catch that blackbird's song?

You know fine well my higher hearing's gone -
controlled explosions and pneumatic drills.

So I try to tune him first to soaring trills
then see-saw notes of warning as the cat
invisibles his predatory self in under-
growth; how the molasses of his song
meanders nightfall when the threat moves on.

Hey look! A golden eagle way up there!

No chance hawk-eye! Marking jotters till dawn.
You know I'm blinder than a cricket ball.

And with his own precision he gives me sun
on the edge of a wind-span throttled back sweet
to find ungainly land in the lee of morning
while I slit my eyes to hear the young call.

The long haul

Just because it's Valentine's Day I do not feel compelled
                 to write a poem about love.
After all it's what we've been for forty years and there's
                 no doubt it brings its own stigmata;
the narrowed finger where your ring has circled freely
the map of laughter lines we've run along together and
those protruding veins that come with sons and daughters.
A pale February sun warms my left shoulder here in our
front room, catches the dust specks a hundred miles away
as you unfold an engineering drawing, build a new day.
You made over-salted sandwiches while I was still asleep,
                 slipped out thoughtful.
I will wash your dishes, make our bed, think about you
from time to time while the afternoon spins by. Start
                 missing you tomorrow.

Portal dolmen

A tomb for the special dead it said
at Poulnabrone and we were quite
alone beside the Pit of Sorrow
pondering there on a cold morning
before the buses and the cameras
swarmed around those ancient hallows.

So I framed you in the stark shape
of megalithic stone that marked the bones
of thirteen beings who must have known
love and light and the heart singing.
I caught the image of that moment
as you turned, smiled. The special living.

Paperwork

So you expect me to collude
against this man who wooed me,
wanted me with such a passion
that it birled my soul tapsalteerie,
tumbrilled my senses wild through
unimagined loops and vacancies?

So you need me to validate
your expert opinion, penned
on sterile sheets and sealed
with cold reason; put our name,
the one we've shared so long,
to this frostbitten treachery?

Well no and no and no again.
I will not snap under the lapses
of his broken memory. We'll thole
till long past bearing when names
are ghosts inscribed on a first kiss
and will-you-marry-me a wish
that once raced through synapses
at the speed of love.

Into care

Old flesh, where indents gradually lose
elastic smiled and frowned in every way
without resilience and spring of youth
to compensate the gouging of the day,
becomes a strange commodity to shift
by wheelchair ramp or zimmer to the new
inspected destination. There a lift
transports their frailness to a heady view,
precision-planted marigolds and grass
they know they cannot access on their own
though nurse and social worker say, "Just ask.
From now on this is where you call your home."
Home smells of memory and risk and mess.
Now they can neatly die in loneliness.

Curtain call

Her father went on a slow-pain ticket
down the single destination line
left her with some money
and a wad of no-more-need-to time.

So she rode the rails of expectation
booked on an occasional plane
took herself farther than she meant to go
beyond the strange epiphany of death
that brought relief and shame,
a new appetite for warm flamboyant sun.

Fun never quite made it
into her noontime tequila
but shadows faltered at the tired corners
of her mouth when she bought
a strappy pair of heels
ready to tap to a new beat.

No call now to make a halo of resentful duty.
There should be years ahead to dance away
from stale exhausted breath
and curtains closed against her day.

ICU

Empty-handed.
That's how you visit here
swiped to the wrists
with clear sterility.
So the orchid, more exotic
than the tricks of science,
will sit by this basement window
catch the best effort of light
our waiting home can give,
attend the silences
the scrape of thank-yous
on the blankest page
that anyone could know.
On the tenth day
I pick a sprig of lavender
calming, healing, able
to draw down summer
from our early days
onto the sleeping pillow.
But they will not let it in.
Perhaps it harbours
the infection of normality
multiplies threats
subtracts small hopes
from those who limbo here
under the lowest rung of life.
Memory is pared down
by the sharpness of now.
I had quite forgotten that
you do not care for lavender.

Dry rot

A smirr of red dust rusty on our kitchen sill.
Serpula lachrymans. So men are here today
to drill, probe, demolish plaster laced
with hair from horses flayed two centuries ago.

A king's hussar, first owner of this place
would have inspected, sounded walls,
swung shutters into measured privacy,
chosen rugs to cosy stone-chilled floors
and caverned wine under cool stairs,
a steep flight to the attic for a maid
who set early fires, twinkled brasses, longed
for a day off to walk the six miles home.

The farrier's son had strong hands,
a ruddy face, laughed with gentle ease
but in her presence all his words had flown.
He shod the horses that her master rode
a white hot craft, radiant and skilled.

Outside the scullery door a cast-off shoe
is hung to augur luck. Spur on hopes. Still.

Lia Fáil

This small karstic stone
lifted in memento
from the rugged pile
we climbed that day
is our Lia Fáil. I knew
it was our destiny,
inaugural as Tara, Scone,
coiled inevitable
in our Celtic knot-work
for the pattern
holds together, closed
in the intricacies
of an unbroken weave.
A homely thing
for a long reign.

Glen Lyon

This day is uisge beatha
distilled out of the glen
through dry stane dykes
and cushion moss and then

this day is widespread wings
as a hawk trusts the sky
to lift him and the shrew
captive in his eye.

This day shepherds a flock
of once unruly sheep
down into the ordered pen
of winter's keep.

This day lingers on the tongue
like muscatel in summer
and on the ear a simple note
of time-worn ways hums.

Ogham

A tiny kirk with fallen sides
and one parabola of rough stone
frames the view. Those who lie below
need no name for earth and sky
have claimed them back to newness.

Beyond I climb the ridged field.
A path is gouged by tractor wheels
deep into mud and boulder, metalled
with cow dung tempered in June heat.

And there it is. I touch the Ogham stone.
It wears white lichen and rose light
for the setting of day. Air rises
rich with the breath of Achamore.

This high place draws the spirit.
No runes remain or plainchant
tuning to the heart but sinners
and the saintly have stood here.

At the tail of evening a low-slung plane
has left violet thinning towards night.
Fair Head and Rathlin settle to the west
and Gigha knows why it is God's Island.

Troon ferry

I love the navy, navy blue
where an eggshell sky
lets the clouds slip through
as far as the furthest wave-top curls.
The shape of the leaving-shore unfurls
and sea-birds parallel the deck
till breakfast's done.

Then they cleave a curve of easy grace
on the chance of an extra bite, no place
for sharing spoils as every feather
quivers towards the sun.

But lead weighs down the scurried skies
on an oil-black sea and the spray is high
as it skims my cheeks with a mist of salt
and expectation

for the Antrim Glens, the hills of Mourne
and Curragh-dreaming foals just born
to graze the drumlins-
glaciated swoops of land grown green
in the hands of calloused centuries, unseen,
where scythes have swung to sow and reap
this complicated nation.

Mahee Island

Ash encircles and a trinity of thorn
all beyond bud but not yet fully grown
to the white flurry of May.
Lough Cuan lies below, spurred with sand
and pearled with small islands.
Silence, the like of which is hard to find
and when I close my eyes the scape
of centuries unfolds into their life.

Monks rough-handed piles of stone,
deep walls to keep this sanctuary
not with the calmness of this afternoon
but hustled full of wattle woven firm
and wood to hew, the raising of a round tower
to fend against the scourge of Vikings.

There were bees to keep and land to till
and sow and reap to feed themselves
and all the souls who sought them-
a fine excuse sometimes for hooleys
and an extra wink of sleep. In the forge
beasts were shod, bells beaten into sound
with brazen tongues to call each man
to prime, terce, sext, none, vespers.

Tenants shared the outer circle of their days
coaxed orchards into succulence of wine
and winter's ample hoard; the surplus
paid the papal tax that bound them.

While scrolling this slowly through my mind
six cars have swung in to park the present.
A gravel-voiced buffoon roars fluent Anglo-Saxon
down his phone, curses the road too winding
and too long, drowns out the blackbird who fills
his orange beak with centuries of song.

Early doors

Five-eighty-an-hour William
day-tripped from the factory,
belly as ballast on the deck,
sun high, sea smooth as a slick
salesman and I'm tuning in.
No siblings, offspring, kin,
just a wraith of loneliness
born a year ago when thrift
and care and love rose skyward
from the local crematorium.

She was crème de la crème
in his café Olé, his only lodestar,
and the coach trips, pale ale
and sympathy of football mates
only filled his mouth with ash,
made a sackcloth for her going.

A bouquet by her headstone
once a week, a room retained
beyond reality, the quiet pain
that masked revulsion at the nudge
and wink replacement therapy-
the wishing well of those
who could not grasp him.

Each night a lock-in tightly turned
to hold the whisperers of change
at bay, linger her essence still
for one more routine day
and then a capsule full of sleep.

Cold night in Tromso.

Some ready to rock and roll
on shore for two short hours.
Others immersed in midnight
murk of floundering dreams.

Then action stations.

Search lights grope concrete
piers, arc under seaweed spaces
where the bridge curves sweet.
Ice cathedral pierces low cloud.

She was just eighteen.

On the first stroke of another day
she chose oblivion. The long jump
before she gulped eternity. No one
went ashore and no one danced.

RIP Sept 2007

Arles

A grove of brushes set in mud-
an old flowerpot, custodian of colour
blooms a sun-bow red, orange, yellow
en garde beside his palette of brown.
They are straight as willow shoots
mop-headed in chrysanthemum
and coltsfoot tossing the thought
of sunflowers thickly daubed
on unrelenting white. Impressive?

No, not quite, for in the corner
of each eye he sees metallic grey
the snub barrel of winter pointing
at his head, shifting his gaze
adrift from the ripening corn
to tune the black caw of crows
across a blank canvas in Auvers.

Image

Was it a fright
or just a curiousity
the first reflection?
He could not tell
his own face, smile,
surprise, frown.

It must have been
the movement-
hands held up,
head bent down
to one side,
finger up nose,
a pose with club.

Light played its part
with this new tantalise,
image screened
on a ripple-splash
or curve to comedy
and early Hammer horror.
It took a while to find
the smoother arts
of preening.

Shall we dance?

That host of golden daffodils-
too much of a coincidence.
They knew a defining moment
when one strolled by
linked to Dorothy and William
on a symbiotic day in Spring.

Samba, salsa, waltz, jive.
Their dancing came alive
with a swagger and a sway,
nothing to do with breeze
or solitary introspection-
just that "X Factor"
urge to seize the sunlight
centre-stage and swing.

An orgasm of earthy bulbs
an orchestra of supple leaves
a collective noun of yellow
strumpeting the dance
gone ding-dong daffodilly
at the Wordsworths' glance
hey-noddy-nodding to the chime
of permanent ink and rhyme.

Owed to poets

A townland in the heart of Derry for Seamus Heaney
                               and the digging of it,
an acorn for Shakespeare from the Birnham wood
                               and the planting of it,
love that wakens to a Skye sunrise for Meg Bateman
                               and the growing of it,
in her own right Rossetti's stall of womanhood
                               and the ripening of it,
Hopkins' the highest rhythm sprung to heaven's gate
                               and the blessing of it,
for Milton the second fruit in Eden's garden shade
                               and the eating of it,
the dearest, greenest place that Edwin Morgan dreams
                               and the savouring of it,
innocence restored to William Blake as each day fades
                               and the experiencing of it.

Astrolabe

Salt on the lips
eyes slitted at the sun
the navigator stands
steady as she lurches
into the green trough.

He often wonders how
someone thought
to cast this metal wheel
etched with nought to ninety
for each of the four winds.

When they rush wayward
through neat symmetry
of clean-cut holes
the mother-board holds fast
against the howling.

On a calm night stars
sharpen their edges
whet their appetite
on her precision,
mark a clear path home.

Orbit

So let us spin
the centrifuge of stars
and skin to skin
frequent the essence
of infinity.
Make it ours.

Thanks to the editors and publishers of the following where some of these poems have appeared previously:

Calder Wood Press; Horizon, Salt Publishing; Magma; Mslexia; Poetry Scotland; Quarrtsiluni; Red Squirrel Press; The Tablet.

I am indebted to Colin Will *(Calder Wood Press)* for publishing my pamphlet "Downside Up" in 2008. My thanks to him, Eleanor Livingstone, Anna Dickie and Kevin Cadwallender for all their encouragement and support and to the School of Poets for good craic along the way.